GARDEN SQUAD!

GROWING VEGETABLES

LOUELLA BATH

PowerKiDS press

New York

Published in 2016 by The Rosen Publishing Group, Inc.
29 East 21st Street, New York, NY 10010

First Edition

Editor: Sarah Machajewski
Book Design: Michael J. Flynn

Photo Credits: Cover, p. 11 Cora Mueller/Shutterstock.com; back cover, pp. 3–4, 6–7, 9–11, 13–15, 17–18, 20, 22–24 (soil) Andrey_Kuzmin/Shutterstock.com; p. 5 gorillaimages/Shutterstock.com; p. 7 (plant) M. Unal Ozmen/Shutterstock.com; p. 7 (roots and soil) Casther/Shutterstock.com; p. 8 SGr/Shutterstock.com; p. 12 Oksana Bratanova/Shutterstock.com; p. 13 nulinukas/Shutterstock.com; p. 15 Julie Vader/Shutterstock.com; p. 16 pukkhoom_nokwila/Shutterstock.com; p. 17 fotohunter/Shutterstock.com; p. 19 HANA/Shutterstock.com; p. 21 Sayanjo65/Shutterstock.com; p. 22 Blend Images/Shutterstock.com.

Library of Congress Cataloging-in-Publication Data

Bath, Louella, author.
Growing vegetables / Louella Bath.
pages cm. — (Garden squad!)
Includes bibliographical references and index.
ISBN 978-1-4994-0973-4 (pbk.)
ISBN 978-1-4994-0997-0 (6 pack)
ISBN 978-1-4994-1014-3 (library binding)
1. Vegetable gardening—Juvenile literature. 2. Vegetables—Juvenile literature. I. Title. II. Series: Garden squad!
SB324.B38 2015
635—dc23

2015010346

Manufactured in the United States of America

CPSIA Compliance Information: Batch #WS15PK: For Further Information contact Rosen Publishing, New York, New York at 1-800-237-9932

CONTENTS

VEGETABLES ARE IMPORTANT 4
WHAT IS A VEGETABLE? 6
GETTING STARTED 10
DIG IN! 12
RAISED BEDS 14
TIME TO PLANT 16
CARING FOR YOUR GARDEN 18
VEGGIE TIME! 20
THE PAYOFF 22
GLOSSARY 23
INDEX 24
WEBSITES 24

VEGETABLES ARE IMPORTANT

Has an adult ever told you to eat your vegetables? Most kids might rather eat sweets, but the adults are right. Eating vegetables is very important. Vegetables have **nutrients** we need to stay healthy. They're also naturally low in calories and fat. Vegetables are one of the best food choices you can make.

There are many kinds of vegetables. One way to become familiar with different kinds is to grow them yourself. Vegetable gardening takes some effort, but the hard work is worth it. Even small gardens can produce months of fresh vegetables—right in your own backyard!

Many gardeners think vegetables are among the easiest plants to grow. Growing vegetables is a great activity for people who are new to gardening.

WHAT IS A VEGETABLE?

Vegetables are plants. Plants have different parts, and each has a special job. Roots keep a plant in the ground. They also take in water and **minerals** that plants need to grow. Roots are connected to a stem, which keeps the plant standing up. Some plants have an underground stem. Water travels through the stem to other parts of the plant.

Leaves take in sunlight and carbon dioxide, which is a gas in the air. Flowers help make more plants. Other plant parts include fruits and bulbs, which are underground buds that store food for plants during winter.

GARDEN GUIDE

Plants use sunlight, carbon dioxide, and water to make their own food. This is called photosynthesis.

These plant parts work together to help plants grow and survive.

A vegetable is the edible part of a plant. If something is edible, that means you can eat it. Vegetables are sorted into groups based on what part of a plant they are. That means when you eat vegetables, you could be eating a root, stem, leaf, bulb, or even flower.

Sometimes vegetables look very different from the way you imagine a plant part would look. For example, carrots, parsnips, and beets are roots. Asparagus and celery are stems. Cabbage and kale are leaves. Broccoli and artichokes are flowers, even though they don't look like it. This **variety** in look, shape, and taste is what makes growing—and eating—vegetables fun!

Tubers are vegetables that are underground stems or large roots. Potatoes and sweet potatoes are tubers. Bulb vegetables include onions and garlic.

VEGETABLE VARIETIES

LEAVES	FLOWERS	TUBERS
CABBAGE KALE BRUSSELS SPROUTS LETTUCES SPINACH	BROCCOLI ARTICHOKES CAULIFLOWER	POTATOES SWEET POTATOES

ROOTS	STEMS	BULBS
CARROTS PARSNIPS BEETS TURNIPS	ASPARAGUS CELERY	GARLIC ONIONS

FRUIT
TOMATOES CUCUMBERS PEPPERS SQUASH EGGPLANT

GARDEN GUIDE

Some plants we call vegetables are actually fruit. A fruit is a plant part that contains seeds. Tomatoes and peppers are common examples of fruits we call vegetables.

GETTING STARTED

The first step in starting a vegetable garden is picking where you want to plant it. Most vegetables need full sun, which means they need to have between six and eight hours of sun a day. Plants that don't get enough light won't produce as many vegetables as you'd like, so pick a sunny spot.

Now that you have the place for your garden, think about how big you want it to be. A good tip is to think small. If your garden is too large, you can have more vegetables than you know what to do with! Starting small is a good way to keep from wasting food.

GARDEN GUIDE

Some vegetables grow well in partial shade. Leafy vegetables, such as spinach, and some kinds of peas can grow without a full day of sun.

Many gardeners plant vegetables in the ground. Gardeners with limited space often grow vegetables in pots. Think about what works best for the space you have.

DIG IN!

The next step in vegetable gardening is preparing your garden beds. The dirt in many backyards isn't good for planting because it may lack important nutrients. It's often too compact, or pressed together, which means air can't flow through it easily. Plants grow best in loose, nutrient-rich soil. You must make sure your garden bed has the best soil possible.

Start by digging your garden bed. Turn the dirt over with a shovel, and break up big chunks with the blade. Now is a good time to add special soils from the store or **compost**. When you've finished, your soil should be loose, **drain** well, and be full of nutrients.

Soil preparation is one of the most important gardening steps.

GARDEN GUIDE

Drainage is very important in vegetable gardening. Your plants' roots will rot, or die, if they sit in standing water.

RAISED BEDS

Many people plant vegetables directly in the ground. However, some gardeners choose to use raised garden beds. A raised garden bed is a garden whose soil rises about 1 foot (0.3 m) off the ground. It's surrounded by walls, which are often made of wood.

Raised garden beds can make vegetable gardening easy. If the soil in your area is poor, you can fill the raised bed with healthy soil. Also, the soil in a raised bed can warm up faster than soil in the ground. This may give you a few extra weeks to garden in the spring and fall.

Once you've built the frame for your raised garden bed, fill it with soil. This is what it should look like when you're done.

GARDEN GUIDE

If you want to garden in a raised bed, you'll need an adult to help you build it. Some stores also sell garden bed kits.

TIME TO PLANT

The best way to choose which vegetables to grow is to think about what you like to eat. That's one way to make sure you enjoy your vegetable garden. Some plants are easy for beginners. Many first-time gardeners have luck with beans, cucumbers, squash, and tomatoes.

The kind of vegetables you grow will affect how you plant them. Most vegetables can be planted in straight rows. Some plants, such as pole beans, need a wall or **trellis** to wrap around as they grow. Every plant is different, so make sure to **research** how to grow them.

PLANTING SCHEDULE

SPRING	EARLY SUMMER	LATE SUMMER
EGGPLANT	BEANS	SPINACH
ASPARAGUS	TOMATOES	LETTUCES
CAULIFLOWER	CELERY	RADISHES
ONIONS	CORN	
PEPPERS	CUCUMBERS	
	SQUASH	

Different seeds need to be planted at different times in order to grow well and produce the greatest amount of vegetables. Every area is different, but here's an example of a planting schedule for New York State.

CARING FOR YOUR GARDEN

You have two choices when it comes to planting: **sowing** seeds directly into the soil and planting seedlings, or baby plants. Growing plants from seeds can be harder than **transplanting** seedlings.

Water your garden well after you've planted it. Cover the seeds and tiny plants with a loose **layer** of straw to keep birds away. With enough sunlight and water, your tiny plants will soon grow into adult plants. Look closely at your plants as they grow. Flowers can be a sign the plant is getting ready to produce food. Can you see tiny vegetables forming?

This plant produced flowers first, then zucchini! It takes about 90 days, or 3 months, for plants to produce fully ripened vegetables.

VEGGIE TIME!

One of the best parts of planting a vegetable garden is **harvesting** all your hard work! Keep an eye on your plants to see when your vegetables are ready to be picked. Color is a good sign of ripeness. Tomatoes and peppers are green at first, but they become very colorful as they ripen.

Size is another thing to look for when harvesting. Don't pick anything too small, because the best flavor comes from having enough time to grow. However, if you don't pick vegetables when they're ripe, they can rot.

GARDEN GUIDE

Give your vegetables a gentle squeeze. Don't pick them if they feel hard. If they feel too soft, they're probably starting to rot.

Many plants respond well to picking. It tells them to produce more vegetables! However, you can only harvest some plants, such as carrots and potatoes, once.

THE PAYOFF

Months of hard work seem worth it when the **reward** is a garden full of tasty vegetables. Growing your own food can bring you a lot of joy. You'll learn a lot about growing plants, and you'll get to try many different kinds of food.

Having a vegetable garden is a great way to connect with nature. It's a great way to stay healthy, too. Make a salad for dinner, or snack on some carrots. Many gardeners will tell you that the food they grow tastes better than what you can buy at the store! Why don't you try it for yourself?

GLOSSARY

compost: Nutrient-rich, soil-like matter that's used to grow plants. Compost can occur naturally, or gardeners can make it.

drain: To allow water or other liquids to pass through.

harvest: To gather.

layer: One thickness lying over or under another.

mineral: Matter important in small quantities for the nutrition of plants.

nutrient: Something a living creature needs to live and grow.

research: To study or look into a subject.

reward: Something earned as the result of one's effort.

sow: To plant seeds.

transplant: To replant in another place.

trellis: A framework of bars used to support climbing plants or trees.

variety: A number of things that are different.

INDEX

B
bulbs, 6, 8, 9

C
carbon dioxide, 6
compost, 12

D
drainage, 12, 13

F
flowers, 6, 7, 8, 9, 18
fruits, 6, 7, 9

H
harvesting, 20, 21

L
leaves, 6, 7, 8, 9, 10

M
minerals, 6

N
nutrients, 4, 12

P
planting schedule, 17

R
raised garden bed, 14, 15
ripeness, 18, 20
roots, 6, 7, 8, 9, 13

S
seedlings, 18
seeds, 9, 17, 18
shade, 10
soil, 12, 14, 18
stem, 6, 7, 8, 9
sun, 6, 10, 18

T
tubers, 8, 9

W
water, 6, 13, 18

WEBSITES

Due to the changing nature of Internet links, PowerKids Press has developed an online list of websites related to the subject of this book. This site is updated regularly. Please use this link to access the list: www.powerkidslinks.com/grdn/vege